KU-351-230

HOW TO BE A MAN

CHABUDDY G.
HOW TO BE A MAN

HarperCollins*Publishers*

Read this book in my woice …

Use your inner woice though …

If you start speaking in my
woice out loud on public
transport you might sound a bit
weird and it might get a little
bit EDL'ish isneet … enjoy, mate!

CONTENTS

'Roses are red wiagra is blue, I faked all of my orgasms* Aldona, so fuck you!'

Chabuddy G, circa 2014, outside Anne Summers, Hounslow High Street

*(For those wondering how a man fakes orgasms, it is done using a very intricate tubing system, yoghurt and some water.)

FOR ALDONA

'It's better to have loved and lost than to have never loved at all' - Some dickhead

People say this all the time but they haven't got a clue, mate. I loved my ex-wife Aldona, and she ended up running away with another man, stealing my beautiful Merc and my most prized possession – my golden foot spa. I loved her but I REALLY loved that golden foot spa. As an athlete (I have athlete's foot, so that makes me an athlete), my feet need special care and no woman has shown my feet love and attention like that foot spa did.

So it might surprise you that I dedicate this book to my ex-wife. Did she break my heart? Yes. Did she treat me like shit? Yes. Did she lie about having six-month-long periods to avoid having sex with me? Yes. Am I over her? YES! I am, like, TOTALLY over her and not bitter AT ALL! I'm totally fine. I'm thriving in fact. Not only am I having loads of sex with, like, proper sexy mums with lip fillers and hard, fake tits, I'm also now a published author. So, fuck you, Aldona, you cow! I don't need you anymore! I'm literally crying AND laughing as I type this. Shaking a bit, too, out of happiness! I AM SO OVER YOU! HOPE YOU ENJOY THIS BOOK WHILE I COUNT MY MONEY HAHAHA!

WHAT DOES IT MEAN TO BE A MAN?
ARE MEN SUPPOSED TO BE FIGHTERS?
LOVERS? SEXUAL ATHLETES?
HUNTER-GATHERERS? FASHIONISTAS?
BUSINESS GURUS? CULINARY
EXPERTS? HOW CAN ONE MAN BE
ALL OF THESE THINGS?
SURELY NO MAN IS A JACK
AND A MASTER OF ALL TRADES?

WELL, I'LL TELL YOU WHAT, MATE,
THERE'S ONE MAN WHO IS ...

He is a girthy geezer from Hounslow, West London, with a silky metre-long ponytail, child-bearing hips and a full-bodied moustache that will make your auntie leave your uncle in a heartbeat, mate. His gold is as fake as the smile you flash your wanker boss. He has many aliases, including:

Alan Brown Sugar, aka Girth Wind & Fire, aka The Brown Casanova, aka The Off-White Bruce Forsythe, aka The Mayor of Hounslow, aka Bombay Beckz, aka The Kebab Shop Heart Throb, aka The Real DJ Khaled, aka Gucci Girls Girth, aka 50 Shades of Brown, aka the Pakistani Peter Andre, aka DJ Vinyl Destination, aka The Girthinator, aka Dhall Boy, aka UKIP'S worst nightmare, aka The Fresh Prince of Hounslow High Street, aka Chabuddy Demus & Pliers, aka Brownton Abbey, aka Bruce Ghee, aka The Armani Arnie, aka Brownadder, aka The Chilli Sauce Bawse, aka Hairy Spice, aka Your Auntie's Favourite Unlicensed Uber Driver.

And many, many more! But the name by which he is best known is Chabuddy G! Aka, me (I sometimes speak of myself in the third person).

In *How to Be a Man*, I will teach you how to be a proper god amongst men. But this book isn't just for the lads. LADY MATES TAKE HEED – these are the qualities you should look for in a heterosexual mate. So, sit back, relax, light a candle. Get naked if you want to. Get the baby oil out – I don't judge. I'm actually naked right now – it makes me more aerodynamic when I type. Although I do keep on sliding off my seat … maybe leave out the baby oil.

How to Be a
Business
Guru

'If a business goes bankrupt
in the middle of the forest and
no one hears it, did that business
even exist? Not according to
my tax records, mate.'
Chabuddy G

This is a true story. In 1998, a young boy saw me balling in my Merc with loads of Polish stunners and asked, 'Chabzy, how can I be a great Business Guru like you?' I told him to get those dried baked bean stains off his top, get a suit and grow some facial hair.

That boy grew up to be Lord Alan Sugar, host of *The Apprentice*.

Now, logically and mathematically this story isn't possible but maths and truth have no place in the business world. I have had many businesses in my time as an ultrapaneer and almost every single one of them has been an epic failure. Has this ever stopped me? No, mate. At this very moment, I have four companies registered and a further three registered under different names, one being 'Alan Brown Sugar'. I treat my businesses like I treat my gold: if they're not worth that much, then I liquidise them. Melt it down, mate – remove all evidence of their existence. No one will know you failed if there's no evidence of you even trying in the first place.

Remember, the most important thing you need in order to become a successful businessman is the ability to lie with supreme confidence. You have to believe in what you're selling, even if you don't believe in it whatsoever.

There are many lies in a single transaction but these lies are beautiful. You're selling your customers happiness – fake happiness, but happiness nonetheless. It's like when I go to a strip club. We all know it's a lie, she doesn't fancy me, I don't love her, but we're all caught up in this beautiful lie, she still gets her 14 pound coins and I still go home with blue balls and a boner. Everyone's a winner!

Business Icons

Now obviously I am the greatest Business Guru of our time but I think it's only fair to give these little geezers a shout-out too. They are brave, inventive and have all made something from nothing, just like me. Look, mate, I came to this country in 1998 with nothing but £5 and my passport. So, let's talk about some of my peers – they've inspired me to an extent but let's be honest, I've probably inspired THEM!

Donald Trump

This orange dickhead is my least favourite entrepreneur. He didn't start with nothing, he comes from money. I do admire the balls on this benchod, though. He is the king of bullshitting and he's bullshitted his way to become the most powerful man in the world. He hasn't got a clue what he's doing as president but one thing's for sure, he's going to make a lot of cash! Let's be real though, we all know he's jacked my style. He's obsessed with gold, has a lot of girth on him and he even has a beautiful Eastern European woman on his arm. He's basically an American Chabuddy G but with shitter hair. If I had to choose one entrepreneur to have a tops-off wrestling match with, it would be this guy. However, a true business guru would never build walls – we build tunnels, mate. Sneak the immigrants in – better for the economy, isneet!

Alan Sugar

I'm not bitter or anything but I've applied for *The Apprentice* nine times and I've been ignored every single time! Why? I'll tell you why, mate. Alan Sugar is shitting his pants and worried that a new ultrapaneer will take over his job – Alan BROWN Sugar! But like I said, I'm not bitter. Keep on selling those little arm stand screens, mate, best of luck to you!!!!!!

Richard Branson

Wow, what a guy. This geezer is the epitome of a Business Guru: he has gyms, trains, planes, broadband, a record label. Even his own bloody island! He even invented cocktails with no alcohol in them! Richie Rich achieved all of this and he's still a bloody VIRGIN! Haha! I think that's why I'm not as successful as him – I have so much sex that it probably distracts me from making more money. Fair play to you, Dicky, you old, rich, virgin bastard!

Job Interview Techniques

I've never had a 9-to-5 in my life. I'm not a sheep, mate. Actually sheep don't have 9-to-5s either but you know what I mean. I'm my own boss. However, I do understand that securing a steady job can sometimes be quite useful … if you're lazy and just want a nice routine, for example, so I'm going to teach you how to get any job you want by mastering the art of the interview. If these techniques don't work, I will guarantee your money back – just fax me SpicybhangraLova69@askjeeves.com. I will reply back within 365 working days.

The Handshake

Instead of the BORING handshake, give this a go: pretend to punch your future employer square in the jaw, but DON'T connect (this is quite important). On the face of it, this looks like a bit of friendly geezer banter but what you've actually done is displayed breathtaking speed and power, leaving a very strong impression that will make you stand out against other candidates. It's called power play. If there is more than one future employer, go for a fake head-butt on the other one. Demonstrate your diverse range of skills.

Eye Contact

Eyes are windows to the soul – that's why you should avoid it at all costs. You don't want them looking into your disgustingly dark, dirty soul. One tip to avoid this is to look anywhere BUT their eyes. I normally look directly into the nipple, even if it's a bloke. Also, try to limit your blinking to three blinks every three minutes – this gives a very powerful and intense 'dead-behind-the-eye' look that employers and Tories love! (most CEOs are Tory scum).

The SHOUT!

This is a classic. I've been using it for years and it works every time. Most of the time. Sometimes. Interviews can get predictable and mundane, so I would recommend that mid-sentence, out of nowhere, YOU START SHOUTING! See, got your attention, didn't I? You know why? Because I shouted mid-sentence, mate. This will startle your employer but also impress them – you're edgy, you're a mentalist. According to academic studies that I've conducted, the loudest person in the room is always the most powerful and the most intelligent.

The Hire Exit

OK, the interview has been going on for a good 15 minutes, your bum is getting clammy, your eyebags are sweating, when will this end? I'll tell you when it'll end, mate, whenever you want! That's right, it's time to learn how to seal the deal with 'The Hire Exit'. Halfway through the interview, get up, don't say anything and just leave. They say first impressions are the most important. Not true. Last impressions are way more important, mate. Always leave them wanting more! This technique works on two levels, firstly you can go outside now and pull your pants out of your arsecrack but secondly it creates an important power shift – it tells the employer that you leave when you want to leave. Are you a dog? Do you follow orders? Sit, get up, shit there, shit here? NO, MATE! You shit where you want to shit, you report to no one. Until you get the job, then technically you will report to your boss.

If you get the job, go to the next chapter. If not, turn the page.

If All Else Fails

So, you've taken my advice and you still didn't get the job. You IDIOT! Now your rent is due, your girlfriend has left you because you're a broke bum and you stink because you can't afford deodorant. Don't worry, mate, shit happens. You obviously didn't follow my advice to a tee, not everyone can be an international business guru like myself.

Every ultrapaneer hits hard times. Trust me, I know – I used to live in my van and shit in a bucket! BUT, and this is very important, as far as anyone could tell I was still as successful as ever. Success is mostly just about how you look. People look at me, they see the ponytail, the jewellery, the shoes ... They know they're looking at a success. So if you have fallen on hard times the best way to deal with it is to just deny it completely and find cunning ways to cover up the crippling financial issues you've been having.

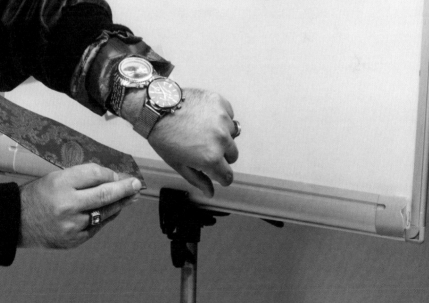

Keeping Up Appearances

Remember, it's all about perception. Sure, my watch is shiny and my rings are blinging – making all the haters cry with envy. But they're not real gold, mate! I just sprayed them gold and tripled the value. To the untrained eye, I look like a bloody Saudi Prince, but look a little closer and you'll see all the green ring marks on my fingers from the fake gold.

Dining

I eat out every single day and I'm not just talking about aural sex. I haven't cooked a homemade meal in 18 years. I'm a gifted chef (see How to Be a Culinary Expert) but I'm too busy making money to cook, mate! But I still eat beautiful food every day, FOR FREE! That's right! I have mastered the art of 'Taster Dining'. I know every spot in Hounslow that hands out free food tasters. All you need to do is wear a disguise every time you go back for more. The other day, I had 17 pieces of the same cheese and I only wore six different disguises! TOO EASY! Bloody idiots!

So remember, guys, you don't have to be a baller to actually be a baller, you just have to look like a baller, and that takes balls, big baller balls. Follow these simple steps and maybe one day you will be a sexy ultrapaneer like me – well, not like me because that's pretty unattainable but you can definitely reach Alan Sugar's pathetic level!! (I will make it on *The Apprentice* one day you old benchod!!!)

how to
be a
fashic

'Dress like a blind man with the confidence
of an attention-seeking peacock.'

Chabuddy G, circa 2012, outside
Blue Inc., Hounslow.

SHOES

After your crotch, the first thing women look at are your shoes, so always stuff your boxers with tissue and always wear sexy shoes. I like boots with a good heel (top tip: don't restrict yourself to the men's section of the shoe shop/stall) – a good heel will make you taller and also create a dramatic, powerful sound when you walk. Sure, it might leave my feet in blisters and sometimes even open wounds, but to be a true Fashionista you must also be a masochist. If it hurts to look THIS good then hurt me baby!

JEWELLERY

Jewellery is very important – why do you think Egyptian pharaohs were buried with all their gold? It's because they knew that even when you die you need to look your best! I rock two fake gold watches at any given 'time' ;) Remember – time isn't real and neither are my watches. These are good-quality fakes, though, I'm not a tramp.

MIX YOUR MATERIALS

Don't be afraid of fabric incest – have a material orgy! Polyester, leather, pleather, nylon, wool, cotton, fur, velour, sheepskin … I have been known to wear all of these fabrics at the same time. I am the Frankenstein of Fashionistas! IT'S ALIVE! No, it's not – it's dead and I'm wearing it!

CLEAVAGE

Fashion is sex. Sex is fashion. It's important to be playful and tease – women have been using cleavage provocatively, making men want more for a millennia. Even the cave women used to show a little tit crease! But hold on a minute, if women can do it, why can't men? When I'm in a club or wine bar I'll lower my trousers to show a bit of cleavage at the back. You can even do it at the front. Open the fly and tease a bit of ball cleavage, maybe even pop a ball out. Don't do this in places where there are prudish bouncers though.

ACCESSORIES

'Before you leave the house, look in the mirror and take one thing off.'
Coco Chanel

With all due respect, Coco, you have no clue about fashion – stick to cereal. I always say that before you leave the house, you should look in the mirror and put at least four extra things on. I'll throw on some tinted sunglasses that colour co-ordinate with my cock ring and my hair band. I have a tie on that's the same colour as my shirt – you can't even see it but I don't give a shit, it's fashion! My belt and boxers are made from the same material – pleather! I'm all about being extra, I WANT to be noticed! I'm a peacock! Accessorise Accessorise Accessorise. Coco you're wrong, madame! If I was a shop, I'd be Claire's Accessories.

ATTITUDE

Being a Fashionista is not just about the things you wear or having millions of people lusting after you, worshipping you like some kind of girthy God, fashion is also about the feel, the wibe, the attitude. The pizza-de-la-resistance of the Fashionista, their secret weapon, is ... the look. Every fashionista worth his crust has his own trademark look. For me, it is the smoulder. A combination of pain and glory. Imagine someone has squeezed a lemon into your eyes and

then punched you in the nuts whilst you're squinting into the distance – this is the smoulder, aka the brown steel. My smoulder can stop people in the street. They will literally come up to me and ask what I'm doing. I'm smouldering,

mate. Get your own look. I look a bit Japanese when I do it too (that's not racist, I'm allowed to say it because I'm from the same continent).

GROOMING

Tache
I use ghee on the tache – keeps it silky and also provides me with a constant aroma of fried foods, mmm.

Ponytail
I wash my metre-long ponytail annually. Hair cleans itself after a while. I'm not sure what shampoo it uses 'cos it does smell quite bad. Sort of like breath. But the perks are that it saves you money in hair products and also the nits keep the mosquitoes away.

Back hair
This has become matted over the years. It takes me 7 hours, 3 mirrors, and 4 bottles of drain unblocker to remove it.

Eyebrows
If you look closely, my eyebrows have the exact same girthiness as my tache, aka my third eyebrow ... #consistency.

Lips
I keep these lubed up at all times with KY Jelly. So much so that I'm often literally dribbling – the ladies love it.

Nose hair
I like to keep my nose hair thick and girthy to filter out any glass or grit when I enjoy a bit of Peanut Dust ;)

Contour
You don't need make-up to contour. I actually shape my stubble to give myself a jawline and cheekbones. To accentuate even further, suck in your cheeks while you talk to people. Trick of the fashion trade, isneet? This can mess your breathing up so keep an asthma pump on you just in case.

DRESSING TO IMPRESS: The Right Outfit For Every Occasion

To be a Fashionista you must also be a chameleon. You must adapt to your surroundings but never conform to what society expects you to wear.

Weddings

So, your best mate is getting married and he's sent you the appropriate attire and colour-way. Pay no attention to this. It might be his big day but this is the perfect opportunity for you to get all the headlines. I went to my Uncle Bobby's wedding dressed in full zebra print – sure I was thrown out but who was the talk of Hounslow the following day? ME, MATE!

First date

Colours are very important for a first date. I always wear a combination of red (the colour of love and also periods – this makes her broody), blue (this symbolises water and leads her mind to hot-tub sex) and gold (this shows that I have money – perfect if you're on a date with a gold-digging slapper. Aldona loved this). The first date is also a perfect opportunity for a bit of ball cleavage. I went on a first date and I had one ball exposed for the entire meal. I took the sexiness one step further by getting the meat balls too. As I ordered I winked at her and looked down towards my crotch – it was nuanced, subtle and classy. She loved it. If she hadn't had to leave because of an emergency and also broke her phone then I was totally in there.

Funeral

You have to be careful with this one as people are emotional and vulnerable. They tell you to wear all black. Why? That's depressing – people are already upset and down. I do the complete opposite – I show up to the

funeral in an all-white tux. Sure, I get funny looks, but in a way this suit is probably what they would have wanted. Let's make funerals sexy again. I'm like a brown angel blessing everyone with my immaculate fashionable outfit, bringing some joy to a pretty shit day. You're welcome.

CASANOVA

'ALWAYS SMELL NICE.
REMEMBER THE FIRST HOLE YOU
PENETRATE IS HER NOSTRIL.'
CHABUDDY G, CIRCA 2002,
OUTSIDE TIGER TIGER.

I'm a fighter. I'm a lover. I'm a lover but I will fight for the right to be a lover and fight you if you try to be my lover's lover unless you're an actual fighter. Confused? Good. Being a Casanova is very complex, it's yin and yang, dark and light – it's all about the perfect balance. The ultimate Casanova is persistent, he will go to any length to secure a lady mate. I once pretended to be gay for three years to get with this sexy Somalian girl who worked in Londis. It didn't work and she still thinks I'm gay. I told her I'm not but she doesn't believe me. I got to see her tits now and again, though, because she was comfortable around me – so I'm still pretty chuffed.

So-called pick-up artists have been conning the world for years with their bullshit techniques that never work. You can't bullshit a bullshitter and I'm the king of verbal diarrhoea, mate, so believe me when I say that I know the secret of keeping a woman happy. But hold on, WHERE THE BLOODY HELL ARE THESE WOMEN? Great question. First we must find our target, our prey, our dartboard, so that we can then start throwing our verbal darts (which sound more painful than they actually are).

FINDING A DATE

THE CLUB

Dark clubs are pretty good places to find a mate, especially if you've got a face like a slapped arse chewing a wasp. I know there's a smoking ban but don't worry about that – walk up to a girl with a cigarette lit, try to blow smoke rings towards her face. It's scientifically proven that women are attracted to the smell of tobacco and beefy BO mixed together. It's very masculine, sexy and old fashioned – reminiscent of alpha males like Clint Eastwood. You might even want to wear a cowboy hat, actually. Clubs can be loud and the less you speak, the less chance you have of screwing up. Express yourself via dance. I recommend the cha-cha, regardless of what music is playing. I once cha-cha'd to drum & bass. Everyone was laughing at me but I still left the club with a fake-tanned 48-year-old STUNNER from Scarborough.

THE SUPERMARKET

So, you got your Mumsy doing the big shop, huh? You bloody caveman! Grow up! It's 2018 – gender roles don't even exist anymore, you tiny man child. The domesticated man is now more desirable than ever. Find your bag for life and get down to your local Tesco's, mate! I would recommend hovering near the tampon section as this shows your feminist side and it's also where you'll find a stream of unexpecting females to speak to. This will be the last place they thought they were going to get lucky! Maybe even pick up a few packets and hand them out as a way to introduce yourself. 'Heavy flow today? Hi, I'm Chabuddy.' It's a great ice-breaker and shows your sensitive, supple side.

If this doesn't work out and you find yourself being escorted from the premises, fear not! Plan B, head to the car park, near the trolleys. As you know, I'm a serial vapist and I blow tonk vapes. As soon as you see a sexy lady park up a trolley, blow a massive vape cloud right in her path. This will leave her disorientated. Next, step through the cloud, smoulder, then introduce yourself. You only get one opportunity to make a first impression and trust me, mate, she will NEVER forget the cool trolley vaping guy.

PUBLIC TRANSPORT

Some people hate rush hour. Not me, and you shouldn't either. It's the PERFECT time to meet women. Imagine this: it's 5:30pm on the central line, everyone's packed in like a can of sardines, mate! A disgruntled beautiful woman who just wants to get home is melting with some fat guy's armpit shoved in her face. Then you show up, with a pocket fan and some wisdom from the Casanova, me, Chabuddy G. You're her knight in sweaty armour. Use your elbows to free up some space around her and then blow her with the fan. Create your own shampoo advert – she's worth it. If this works and she is feeling less hot and bothered, spark up a conversation. The great thing about packed trains is that she can't leave – she's your sexy prisoner and you're her own personal air-conditioning unit. If you pull, remember to mind the gap – HER GAP! Am I right, lads? ;)

JOB CENTRE

This is a hidden gem. The best place to meet women is actually the Job Centre. I like a woman who's desperate – it works to my advantage. She's run out of options, she's fed up, she'll take anything she can get ... BAM! That's where I come in. You get all types of women at the Job Centre – exotic foreigners who can't speak English very well (loads of raunchy Romanians), council estate mums (very sassy, my personal favourite) and even posh, snobby colonial bloodline women called India and Poppy. Daddy has cut off their allowance and they really, really want to get back at him by humping an ethnic. This is your chance to be their new sugar daddy, but with less money ... artificial sweetener daddy, if you will.

Relationships

OK, so you've found your girl and now you've started a relationship. Congratulations, mate, but this is where it can get tricky. You can't get lazy – just because you've thrown your rod out into the ocean and caught your fish doesn't mean that you should stop and go back home and put your feet up and eat the fish. That fish is your girlfriend now and she needs to be looked after. Here are some tips to keep your relationship fresher than my uncle who just arrived here last week on a bloody banana boat, mate!

TEXTUAL HEALING

Women love texts. Show your woman that you care by texting her loads of cute things like 'Miss you babbbiiii xxxx' and 'Can't wait to kiss you, honey tits xoxoox' and 'Where the fuck are you??? Who are you with??!! hehehehe xxxxx'.

GETTING AWAY

We all need a break now and again. Sometimes life can be like groundhog day – same shit, different toilet. It's time for you and your lover to get away. There are countless romantic locations around the world to choose from. How about you take her to smelly Venice and eat a gondola while renting a gelato? Or take her to Paris and eat some frog dick or whatever they eat over there! Can't afford any of that? Don't worry, mate. Why don't you take her to Southall, West London – aka Little India. It's wonderfully overcrowded with brown people and curry so racists hate it but your girlfriend will LOVE it. Unless she's also a racist, then I would recommend somewhere up north.

COMMITMENT

Things are getting really serious now. You're in a long-term relationship but things aren't going too smoothly. You hardly talk, you haven't had sex in months, you hate each other's company, she's probably cheating on you with the new gorgeous Greek guy from accounts. There's only one thing to do. Pop the question! It's the ultimate show of commitment, the grandest gesture! Now you can be securely trapped together in matrimony FOREVER! If that doesn't work, try and at least get her pregnant. As long as you've got her tied into something permanent then the happiness thing will eventually probably sort itself out.

PICK-UP LINES

'Hey, baby, black don't crack and beige don't age.'

'Hey, was your great-grandfather in the British Raj, cos you look like you have some Indian in you. Want some Pakistani in you too?'

'You like dipping in the chocolate, baby tits?'

'Hey, sugar face, wanna make some beige babies and live the UKIP nightmare?'

Note: These lines will only work for the Asian lads.

HERE'S SOME UNIVERSAL ONES THAT HAVE WORKED FOR ME IN THE PAST.

'All I got for you is hard dick and bubble gum and I'm all out of hard dick bubble gum.'

'Hey, I'm a time traveller come back in time to tell you that you should go out with me 'cos the future of the world depends on it. Jump in the Merc.'

'Can I buy you a drink? I've heard there's a lot of date rapists around these parts so I am protecting you.'

'Did you fall out of the sky because you look like an angel and also you have a bruise on your arm.'

CHIRPSING TEKKERS

Now I know this technique has been around for some time but people have been doing it wrong. I have invented a new style called 7 down 1 up. You viciously insult the lady seven times, then give her one compliment and hand over your phone number. Like this:

'Hi there. Your eyes are too close together, your lips look like fish lips, you look like your bra smells, I can see your nose hairs when you laugh, you look like a clown with all that make-up, you haven't got the legs to wear skirts, your breath smells like pot noodle and hash. BUT I like your shoes, give me a call.' Never fails.*

*It fails sometimes.

SEND A GIRTH CERTIFICATE (DICK PIC)

Sending sexy, enticing photos to girls is an art form. Don't go straight in with the dick pic. I like to use a two-prong approach, a double-ender if you will. For my first Girth Certificate I use a fake bank statement. Show that you got millions in the bank so she knows you're a real boss. Once you've got her all excited it's the perfect time to bring her back down to earth with a real dick pic. She'll still be thinking about that bank statement and won't even notice that your penis is below average size and a slightly strange colour. It's a win win.

YOUR SONG

I would recommend picking 'your song' before you even meet your date. That way when you're shit-faced you can say 'Oh my God, sweetie face, it's our song, let's start dirty dancing isneet!' She might be confused at first but just go with it. I would recommend 'Pony' by Ginuwine because it has some really excellent hidden metaphors about her riding on your penis. I don't know what the saddle he talks about is supposed to represent, maybe a condom.

LIPSING

The first kiss is also very important on a first date, luckily for you lot I have the perfect technique. First of all make sure you eat something garlicky before, you want the first kiss to be very memorable and a strong aroma will do this. Count how many times she licks her lips, if it's more than 3 times in a minute then she's ready for a snog, mate. Close your eyes, tilt your head, bite your lip, then open your mouth really wide and stick your tongue out (roll your tongue if you can), lean towards her very slowly, works all the time.

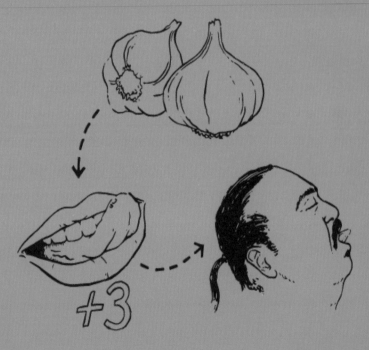

+3

Disclaimer: This doesn't work all of the time, you might get a slap but at least you gave it a go, women like a risk taker.

CHABZY'S FINAL THOUGHTS

The most important part of a relationship is dirt. Make sure you have enough dirt on your partner so they never even dream of leaving you or cheating on you. It's like the Cold War – you both have your missiles pointed at each other, just waiting, always under constant threat. It keeps the relationship sexy, fresh, dangerous, and it's a really intense way of keeping the passion alive. I tried to use this technique on my Polish ex-wife, Aldona, but being from Eastern Europe she was wise to the Cold War tactic. She flipped it on me and actually ended up robbing, leaving, and cheating on me. The Big Three! I kind of respect her for it, the beautiful evil whore!

LADIES' APPRECIATION PAGE

There are a lot of disgusting men out there. So much hatred and misogyny. But there's one thing that brings us all together – vagina. I don't discriminate, mate. Every race, culture, and creed has hot chicks that I would love to bang. I think the world should just have one massive orgy and we should all cum together, literally. So, here's a dedication to all the sexy mamacitas across the globe. Chabuddy loves you all. Even the unattractive ladies out there – to me you're sexy anyways, baby.

Shout out to all my Angelic Armenians • Big up all my Busty Bosnians • Winky face to my Curvy Croats • Heyyyy to all my Decadent Danes • Love to my Elegant Ethiopians • I want to kiss you my Feisty Finn • Large up my Girthy Ghanaians • Horny Haitians • Indecent Indians • Juicy Jamaican • Kinky Kosovons • Luscious Lithuanians • Mucky Mongolians • Naughty Nigerians • I still remember you, all the Orgasmic Chicks who were in the Ottoman Empire • Perky Pakistanis • Quintessential Qatarian • Raunchy Romanians • Sexy Somalis • Tantalising Thais • Unique Uruguayans • Voluptuous Venezuelan • Wicked West Indians • (Can't think of any countries beginning with X so will just give you kissies xoxoxooxoxox) • Shout out all my fancy former Yugoslavs • Zingy Zimbabweans

HOW TO BE A CULINARY EXPERT

'THE WAY TO A WOMAN'S HEART
IS DIRECTLY DOWN HER THROAT.'

CHABUDDY G, CIRCA 2014, IN ALADDIN'S
FRIED CHICKEN SHOP, HOUNSLOW.

FOOD FOR THOUGHT

The NHS will have you believe that a lady's G-spot is located near her arsehole. This isn't true. It's actually located in her stomach, and the way to truly please your woman is through food. It's important for a man to know his way around a woman's special parts, but more importantly, around the kitchen. I'm a foodie, mate. I was literally born in the kitchen, back in Lahore, on the floor – my dad made a curry out of my mum's afterbirth, aka the aftergirth. They wouldn't admit it themselves, but I have actually inspired some of the nation's greatest chefs.

MARY BERRY

There's something about Mary! Trust me, mate! Off the record, we actually had a whirlwind romance back in 1996. You know I like a mature woman and she was my Mrs Robinson for a bit. We used to cook together. Remember that scene in *Ghost* with the clay? We did that but with a massive kebab skewer, it was so hot, so intense, so greasy! I used to serve her peanut dust cookies in bed – this is what inspired the idea for *Bake Off*. I was supposed to present it with her but they said our sexual chemistry on screen was too steamy for pre-watershed TV. Miss you, baby. x

GORDON RAMSAY

Gordy came to my restaurant back in the day and asked for something off-menu. I served him a gourmet kebab coulis after a frozen chilli sauce and garlic amuse bouche. He had the shits for two weeks afterwards but he praised me for my courage and creativity in the kitchen. After that, the shouty prick stole my whole style and got his Mitchell and stars.

JAMIE OLIVER

Everyone knows Jamie and his restaurant, Jamie's Italian. Here's an industry secret that not many people know. Jamie isn't actually Italian! He's a fraud, mate! Next time you see him, say something to him in Italian and look at his confused little liar expression. I'm on to you, Jamie!

CHABZY'S RECIPES

They say men are the best chefs. This isn't true and I'm sure a man came up with this lie. Ugh, men are the WORST! Am I right, ladies? However, men do tend to be riskier than women when it comes to food. The kitchen is like a science lab to me and trust me, mate, I like to experiment! Whether it's food or sex I am ready to break down all the boundaries to ensure that my customers are satisfied. Actually, that sounded weird, I'm not a prostitute. But I will take your cash and make your dreams come true.

Medium-rare Hearty Chicken with Crunchy Peanut Dust Roast Potato and Beef Monster Munch

1. Get a whole chicken and wash it. Don't worry about taking out all the stuff inside (like the heart or liver) – leave that in, it adds flavour.

2. Marinate the chicken in its own blood. This adds character and helps to remind you that this bird died for you.

3. Using the garlic cloves, fist the chicken. Get deep in there. If you're struggling to get your fist in, use whatever lubricant you have to hand.

4. Preheat the oven to 220 degrees and bung the bird in.

5. To prepare the potatoes, firstly remember not to wash your hands – it's nice to infuse them with the raw chicken flavour. This brings the dish together, it's part of the narrative.

6. Drown your potatoes in ghee and peanut dust – this will make them extra crunchy when roasted. Watch out for any glass in the peanut dust, and ideally remove it.

7. Take your chicken out after 13 minutes. What you're looking for is white skin on the outside and a thin layer of pink on the inside. All the foodies know that medium-rare* is the best way to eat your chicken!

8. Serve your chicken and potatoes on a plate with a handful of beef monster munch on the side.

9. Mmm, now tuck in!

*Disclaimer – only eat medium-rare chicken if, like me, you can digest raw meat. If you can't, I would recommend cooking for 17 minutes so that it's medium-well done.

Mystery Meat Mondays

1. Go to the butcher on a Monday. Say, 'I'd like a pick'n'mix bag please, Chabzy sent me.' Wink three times and stick out your tongue for three seconds. You have just activated the secret pick'n'mix mystery meat gift pack. Every butcher in the country knows this code. They will give you something 'off-menu' from the back of the shop. It will be in a black bag.

2. When you get home, empty the meat into a searing-hot pan, preferably whilst blindfolded.

3. The aroma from the mysterious meats might be unusual, even a little sickening, but this is all part of the fun!

4. Throw in some onions and turmeric. Now the stench will be even more intense! Reduce to a low heat and simmer for six hours.

5. Invite some friends over to play 'Mystery Meat Mondays!' Is it veal? Is it hedgehog? Is it squirrel? Is it cat? You'll never know. That's what makes this dish so edgy and traumatic but also cute and fun!

6. Bury all the leftover meat in your garden as some of the meat may not technically be legal. You have just completed Mystery Meat Monday! Congratz!

Blue Velvet Cake

Now it's time for dessert! This cake is something I've been making for years and it's a real winner, no matter how 'stiff' the competition is! Can be eaten alone or with a partner.

1. Get some Viagra.

2. Pour milk, flour and eggs into a mixing bowl.

3. Take one Viagra for inspiration and then pour the rest into the mix before beating with a wooden spoon.

4. Bake for 40 minutes or until golden brown.

5. Serve the cake immediately. Do not allow it to cool. As you eat, you will realise that your tongue will start to stiffen, therefore enhancing the flavours and guaranteeing you multiple mouthgasms.

COCKTAILS

You're stuffed from all that beautiful food but now you're bloody parched! You need something to wash it down, so how about some cracking cocktails? I used to be pretty sick on the decks – they called me DJ Vinyl Destination. Making cocktails and DJing are very similar, hence the word mixologist, isneet! Here are some of my personal favourites. Give them a try!

Peanutini

This is my take on the classic Martini. I think the world is ready for an Asian Bond, too! The name's G, Chabuddy G.

1. Find a pint glass.

2. Pour a pint of Polish vodka in.

3. Add 3 shots of tequila (might overspill).

4. Add 2 tablespoons of salt and pepper.

5. Finish with crushed peanut dust around the rim, mmm crusty rim.

6. Set on fire.

7. Shake AND stir to put the fire out. Enjoy!

Micro COCKtail

It's not all about size, mate! Length is overrated. It's all about girth. Remember, sometimes the smallest things pack the mightiest punch!

1. Get an egg cup.

2. Pour in 100%-proof alcohol.

3. Find the tiniest aubergine you can.

4. Using a straw, pump the aubergine full of vodka lassi and create an opening on the tip of the aubergine.

5. Place the aubergine into the egg cup.

6. If done correctly, the aubergine should squirt in your face when you drink this little potent firecracker.

The Brexit Brandy

This is a drink guaranteed to bring us all together and to make racists FUMING! It's a brandy cocktail with a little bit of immigrant flair.

1. Get a pint glass.

2. Pour a pint of Romanian brandy into the glass.

3. Add a teaspoon of turmeric and curry powder.

4. Add a handful of finely chopped Somalian Chad.

5. Add some beetroot from your local Polski Sklep.

6. Finish off with a sprinkle of West African Jollof rice.

7. Serve to a racist to teach them how to appreciate different cultures – all via a delicious cocktail!

HOW TO BE A
HUNTER-

'We're so dependent on our gadgets, what if the robots take over and we all end up being bummed by Florence and her machine? We must go back – go back to the essence of MAN.'

CHABUDDY G, CIRCA 2015,
AT THE SELF-SERVICE CHECKOUTS AT ALDI.

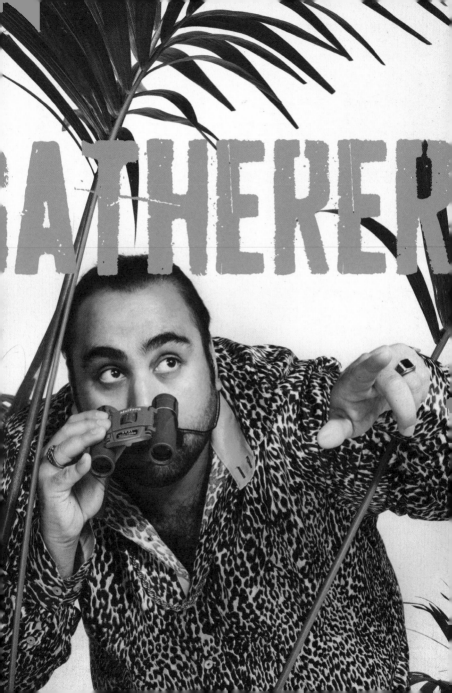

PICTURE THE SCENE: IT'S 2028.
POST-BREXIT BRITAIN IS NOW A THIRD-WORLD
COUNTRY. TRUMP IS STILL PRESIDENT (HE'S
HALF ANDROID, HALF DICKHEAD). THERE'S ONLY
ONE LONDIS LEFT IN LONDON. FOOD IS SPARSE,
YOU MUST HUNT TO EAT – IT'S LIKE THE BLOODY
HUNGRY GAMES OUT THERE, MATE! DON'T WORRY,

YOU WILL SURVIVE. JUST FOLLOW MY TIPS ON HOW TO GET BY WHEN THE SHIT HITS YOU IN T FACE (LITERALLY, HUMAN SHIT WILL BE ALL THAT THERE IS TO USE AS AMMO IN THE FUTU

SURVIVAL BASICS

BE A FIRE STARTER, A TWISTED FIRE STARTER

A true Hunter-gatherer will know that the first thing you must do is start a fire. It will be your most essential tool for staying alive – it gives you heat, light and food. It's also good for telling spooky stories. Here's how you start a fire from scratch.

1. Gather wood.

2. Gather a lighter.

3. Use lighter to light the wood.

4. If the lighter doesn't work, gather matches and use them.

5. If it's windy, ask a friend to help you.

6. Even better, ask him for a lighter.

7. Tell a spooky story and stay warm.

ALL YOU NEED IS LOVE, AND SHELTER

Besides the zombie crackheads that want to eat your flesh and the genetically modified illuminati tomato humans, the Hunter-gatherer's biggest enemy is the elements. Girth, wind and fire, baby, they're killers! You MUST get a roof over your head ASAP.

1.   Find a shelter.

2.   Enter it.

DESPERATE TIMES, DESPERATE MEASURES

If you don't eat, you die! It's simple, mate. This is where you must employ all your hunter-gathering skills. I once got lost on Hounslow Heath for three hours and to survive, I had to catch and eat three butterflies, two ladybirds and two eggs that I found in a bird's nest. I didn't want to do it but when push comes to shove, sometimes you have to eat what Mother Nature provides, even if it is traumatic and then you find your way out minutes later and regret it.

CUM IN A CUP
Bear Grylls is a complete idiot. He hasn't even been alone in the wilderness – there's always a cameraman with him! He's always drinking his own piss and inhaling his own farts but he's got it wrong, mate. Urine does nothing for you, but semen is very good for you – it's a natural oxidant, great for the skin and can keep you going for days! Spit or swallow? If you want to live, always swallow! So, next time you're in need of a boost, don't drink your own piss, just cum in a cup. Cheers! (I would recommend eating pineapple before, definitely not asparagus or fish.)

FIND IT, KILL IT, EAT IT, WEAR IT
Hunting isn't just about eating, though. Sometimes you must kill to look good. Even if you're starving and living in your own shit, that's no excuse to look like a tramp! I want to leave a stylish-looking corpse, so if you do kill a hedgehog, eat the meat, sure, but keep the skin and make some sexy spiky shoes. Kill a tortoise, make a hat. Kill a chicken, make a chicken-skin bag. Use your imagination. The majority of the world might be dead but that doesn't mean fashion has to die too.

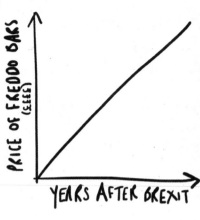

PRICE OF FREDDO BARS (£££)

YEARS AFTER BREXIT

TRADING

I've always been a hustler, mate, two steps ahead of the market. Sterling? Euros? Bitcoin? Ha! More like shitcoin! All useless, mate! In this post-apocalyptic world, we will return to the age-old practice of trading. Here are some of my predictions for items that will one day be of high value and will all be great trading commodities!

PLEATHER
I ONLY wear pleather. Why? Because a good pleather jacket will be worth a lot as it's multipurpose. It looks great but it's also strangely edible and will last for days because it's very, very chewy.

FREDDO BARS
In the years after Brexit, one single Freddo bar will be worth up to £750. They will be like gold dust! I have bought eight thousand boxes and frozen all of them in anticipation. Can't wait to cash in!

HOW
TO BE A
FIGH

'You must be shapeless, formless, like peanut dust. When you pour peanut dust into a cup, it becomes the cup. When you pour peanut dust into a bottle, it becomes the bottle. When you pour peanut dust into a teapot, it becomes the bloody teapot, mate! Peanut dust can drip and it can crash. Become like peanut dust, my friend.'

CHABUDDY G, AKA BRUCE GHEE, CIRCA 2003,
OUTSIDE GOLDS GYM, GREENFORD.

This quote doesn't make any sense but I haven't been paid that much to write this book so I needed to plug my product, Peanut Dust. I have 400 boxes left, they're stagnating and I really need petrol money. Contact to purchase: SpicyBhangraLova69@askjeeves.net

I've been fighting my whole life, geezer! I came out of my mum's vagina doing jungle jiu-jitsu and using the umbilical cord as bloody nunchucks, mate! Although I have a very friendly face I am a VERY dangerous man. My street-fighting record is 428-1, that one defeat was to myself – I got smashed on the vodka lassis and started punching myself to show people my power and accidentally knocked myself out. I actually don't fight anymore, my hands are registered weapons and it just wouldn't be fair to the other guys I'm fighting. I'm basically the Hounslow Thanos; you know, that massive geezer from Avengers with the Jimmy Hill chin? Violence is NEVER the answer but sometimes if another man attacks you or your family then you just gotta throw down, mate! We all have an animalistic rage inside of us, we want to fuck and fight – sometimes at the same time! Here's some excellent tips on how to be a fighter, including some of my secret jungle jiu-jitsu moves. This is a type of martial arts that I invented in Lahore and then perfected on the piss-stained streets of Hounslow (the piss is from the geezers I fought because they pissed themselves, isneet).

CHABUDDY G SPECIAL TECHNIQUES

THE
PILLOW
FIGHTER

SKILL	2/10
EFFECTIVENESS	6/10
STREET CRED	0/10
BRUTALITY	1/10

THE WORLD IS YOUR WEAPON

People talk about fair fight this, fair fight that! Listen, don't worry, it's all fair in love and war. If you have an advantage over your opponent, use it. A cheap shot is still a shot and every shot counts when you're fighting. Use what you have available. If you're wearing a nice bulky watch, smash him in the face with it, blind him with the bling, if it's fake gold that's even better, it will leave him with green bruises!

Use your surroundings

I was once in a road-rage incident where I refused to get out the Merc. You can't beat a man who has a car as a shield. Yes, some people might say that's cheating but I drove away without a scratch. Apart from on the Merc, that was actually really badly damaged.

Use your imagination

Say you're in a pub and it's about to kick right off. All you have around you is olives on sticks. Fashion a Wolverine-like toothpick glove out of the olive sticks and punch him in the ball sack – get creative! I once got in a fight in a furniture store because some perv was eyeing up my Aldona. I actually knocked him out using only pillows. It was the most vicious pillow fight you'll ever see, he awoke from his slumber, covered in piss like, 'Ahh, Chabuddy G, not fucking with him again.'

WEIRD HIM OUT

Sometimes your opponent will be much bigger and stronger than you. I can fight for a maximum of 13 seconds at my optimum speed before I gas out, after that I'm in trouble. This technique is perfect when your back's against the wall, you're out of breath and you need a Get Out of Jail card.

It's called 'weird him out, mate'. I once got in a fight with a 6-foot-7 Albanian meathead over some credit card fraud, he was absolutely battering me, so what did I do? I took my trousers off and soiled my pants. He was baffled. I then ran around flinging my shit at him and

making chimpanzee noises.
Let's just say he didn't bother
me ever again. Sure, I got
sectioned for a couple of days
but my rep as a raging lunatic
was secured on the streets of
Hounslow. There's other ways
you can weird them out too:
put your fingers in their belly
button, not in a weird way just

to confuse them. I sometimes
start speaking in tongues and
hitting myself – this will
create the illusion that you've
been possessed. Once again, it
may get you sectioned so use
it sparingly.

REVERSE CINDERELLA SPIN

I'm a fashionista, I'm known to be very experimental with my outfits, I even wear women's boots sometimes. This isn't a kinky thing, women's boots have great heels on them. This is great for two things: making you look taller and for doing my favourite fighting move – the Reverse Cinderella Spin! This move was invented when I was trying on women's shoes in Clarks and some geezer called me a tranny. I did a 360° spin and used the heel on the boot to kick a Slush Puppie out of his hand. He took one look at me and knew I was kung fu fighting and that I was as fast as lightning (like the song, isneet). It was too much for his brain to process so he just apologised to the saleswoman about the Slush Puppie and walked out. Afterwards the saleswoman told me that he hadn't called me a tranny, he was actually from up north and was saying the word 'trainers'. Still, he learnt not to mess with Chabuddy G that day. Borrow your girlfriend's or your mum's boots and try this move at home – heels must be a minimum of 6 inches long, stilettos are also fine.

REVERSE CINDERELLA SPIN

SKILL   9/10
EFFECTIVENESS   10/10
STREET CRED   6/10
BRUTALITY   8/10

THE TICKLER

I used to play a sport in Pakistan called Kabaddi. It's like a combination of rugby, wrestling and tag. This is actually how I got my name, Chabuddy, because I was a 'G' at Kabaddi and it rhymes, isneet? The Tickler is a move I learnt whilst playing Kabaddi. Sometimes it's not all about punching, 95% of fights end up on the floor. This is where my jungle jiu-jitsu skills become very helpful. When in a grappling situation, tickle your opponent, go for the back of the neck, under the armpits, soles of the feet, balls, even use your tongue (not on the balls). This is also one of the many reasons why I have a girthy tache, it's a perfect tool to perform The Tickler (the ladies love it too). I have made grown men cry from nuzzling into their neck with my tache. Very underrated move!

THE TICKLER

SKILL	10/10
EFFECTIVENESS	8/10
STREET CRED	10/10
BRUTALITY	8/10

THE BELLY BUTTON JAB

SKILL	9/10
EFFECTIVENESS	10/10
STREET CRED	6/10
BRUTALITY	8/10

We interrupt this book for a political party message brought to you in part by the Beige Party.

Politics is the biggest pantomime ever staged. 'Oh no it isn't!' Oh yes it is, mate. Politicians are just actors on a stage, reading from a script. And we've all heard the script before, it's the same bloody bullshit lies coming out of their wealthy little arsehole mouths. Now is the time for someone fresh to step up with some new ideas, a new script that I will just make up as I go along. It's time for a new type of politician. Me, Chabuddy G! I won't lie to you. I'm openly corrupt, I'll tell you that I'm going to con you. I'm being truthful about being dishonest.

VOTE FOR CHABUDDY G

'MORALS AND POLITICS DON'T MIX, LIKE TWO GUYS AND NO CHICKS. UNLESS YOU'RE GAY, IN WHICH CASE THEY DO MIX, AND MORE POWER TO YOU, MATE.'
– CHABUDDY G, CIRCA 2016, SPEAKING TO A CRACKHEAD OUTSIDE HMV.

THE HOUSING CRISIS

London is absolutely chockablock! Everyone wants to come to the big city and chase their dreams! The problem is it costs 1k to basically live in the equivalent of a shed. Then it hit me, if you're gonna live in an equivalent to a shed, why not an actual shed, mate? Let me introduce 'Bed in a Shed'. For the last four years I have been renting out Beds in Sheds all over London, some in Bradford too. Here's how it works, empty out all the gardening tools from your shed and concrete over the grass so it's easy to maintain. Next make a bed on the floor by chucking down a few old blankets, then find a desperate person and move them into your shed! Charge them £250 quid a month, £15 extra a month for the fox repellent equipment (a lighter and a can of Lynx), and only £5 extra for torch batteries. You won't find prices like that anywhere else in London, even if it is zone 6! They can log into your wifi from the garden and get decent one-bar signal. Still trying to work out the whole water and toilet situation but, you know, baby steps. Bed in a Shed will solve the housing crisis!

VOTE FOR CHABUDDY G

FOR RENT

BREXIT

I never normally pull out because I fire blanks, so it was a bit of a shock to me when we pulled out of the EU. It doesn't really affect me because I'm technically not even a real person, I haven't even got an NI number, haha! But I am a bit worried for my sour-faced Eastern European ice queens! What if I can't get any more potent Polish princesses? A world without immigration is a world without Aldonas, and I for one will not stand for it! I want to introduce 'SEXIT' – it's like Brexit but we only let in fit

VOTE FOR CHABUDDY G

Europeans and then we all have sex! I will appoint myself chief immigration officer and I will be VERY hands on with what types of women we are letting into our country. Also, I promise to keep Toblerone normal-sized, Space Raiders will be 10p again, 1-penny sweets will be 1p again, and Britain will be great again!

THE NHS

The NHS is brilliant and we are very lucky to have it, a lot of my brown people run that shit, so you're welcome. But the NHS is also under a lot of pressure and I have the perfect solution. Three words: Le-Ga-Lise. I would first of all make the devil's lettuce aka reggae spinach aka weed available on the NHS, it will chill everyone out. Alcohol-related injuries are one of the biggest burdens on the NHS. Imagine if everyone was smoking weed! When was the last time you heard of someone getting injured by playing FIFA with their top off and talking about 9/11 conspiracies, mate? It almost never happens. Also, sales of Pringles and Capri Sun would go through the roof, thus helping the economy! You can't spell healthcare without THC. I would also hire sex workers to be part of the NHS, free on delivery! Depression is a big problem in this country, my plan is to make the sex workers qualified therapists so if you're feeling a bit down you can get noshed off and then talk about your trauma. Very therapeutic!

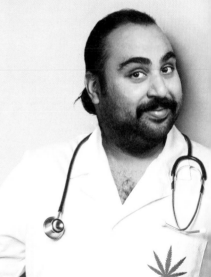

THE RAINBOW PASSPORT

To tackle immigration I would take an extreme yet very humane action. I would abolish our boring red (soon to be blue) passports and I would introduce the rainbow passport. This will make you a citizen of planet Earth. Not just one country, we are all part of one race, mate, the human race. You will be able to roam free and spread your seed to whomever you want! Mix all the races and cultures up until we all become beige. The future is beige, mate!

HOW TO BE A MILLENNIAL MAN

'Real men have curves!'

— Chabuddy G, circa 2014, in Primark complaining
to the staff because none of the shirts fit.

Man is evolving. In the past, the only time a man was allowed to express his emotions was when screaming with tears in his eyes at a football game, or beating the shit out of someone outside a kebab shop at 3am. This has all changed now. A new man has emerged – the Millennial Man: he is a sensitive, nuanced soul with an open, emotional girth hole that is gaping and begging to be filled ... with LOVE. He talks about his feelings and treats women with respect, he is upset and offended by everyone and everything, he recycles and does yoga and vapes. I am that new man and I can teach you how to be that new man too. Grab some tissues and play some Enya in the background – you're in a safe zone now, bro. x

❤ 69 likes

 chabuddy_g Looking sexy mate, would defo bang 👌 👅 🔥

chabuddy_g Cheers mate, you looking tonk too! Love you xx

❤ 69 likes

chabuddy_g dreamy! 😏 hehehehe

OCEAN OF EMOTION

I remember my old man would never cry. I thought that was normal but it's not! Men should express their emotions. It's essential. There's two things I know about real men; they have curves and they cry. When Aldona left me I would not only cry but I would combine it with a wank in an attempt to show her that I didn't need her and I'm fine on my own. These cry-wanks are also known as cranks. It's very healthy and

very empowering and you don't need lube as the tears provide lubrication.

#SelfLove is very important for the Millennial Man. I make love to myself on a daily basis (I'm not talking about wanking anymore but actually that is part of it). Give yourself a pat on the back, buy yourself a present, send YOURSELF nudes! Slide into YOUR OWN DMs, like YOUR OWN pictures on Instagram, even leave a little

♥ 69 likes

chabuddy_g fuck aldona, look what she'
xxxxx ♥

♥ 69 likes

chabuddy_g 2 hot 2 handle babe xxxxxx 🔥🔥🔥

cheeky comment like 'Looking sexy mate, would defo bang :aubergine emoji:' Or, 'Hey man saw that pic you put up, you looking sexy geezer!' I'd then wait a few days (don't want to come off needy) and reply like, 'Cheers mate, you looking tonk too! Love you xx'. It's little things like this that keep you happy, express your emotions, mate! No one's gonna love you if you don't love yourself! Sing like no one's listening, have sex like no one's filming! I wake up every morning, look in the mirror and just sing my name (to the rhythm of the White Stripes – 'Seven Nation Army') like 'Ohhhhh Chabuddyyyy Geeeeeeee'. Try this yourself, it's like a therapeutic mantra, maybe even throw it in when you're making love to yourself (OK, now I am talking about wanking).

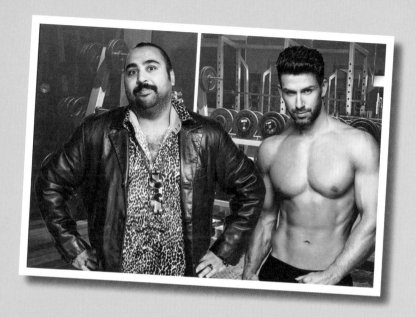

LOVE THE SKIN YOU'RE IN

Six packs are very overrated. Girls don't even like them anymore, there's too many of them. They're bloody everywhere. I'm not working on my summer bod, I'm actually working on my winter bod, loads of carbs before Marbs, mate! It's easier for me as I've had girth from birth, but to all the young geezers out there at the gym, forget about it, stay at home. Ladies don't want those chiselled abs anymore, they're sharp and they hurt, it's like hugging a pile of really sexy bricks. Women want something to hold on to when cuffing season begins. Hugging me is like snuggling a massive hairy pillow. Regardless of what shape you are, if you like it then that's all that matters. There's nothing sexier than a confident person who loves the skin they're in. I'm normally in leopard skin and I love it!

BE ANY MAN YOU WANT TO BE!

I know this book is called *How to Be a Man* but in order to be a Millennial Man you basically have to ignore my advice. What's he talking about?? That's for you to figure out, mate. Don't listen to me, the Millennial Man doesn't conform to what society or anyone else tells him! Back in the day the man would be the breadwinner and the woman would stay at home, cook, clean, raise the kids, and have an affair with the milkman. This is an archaic way of living, why can't the man stay at home and have an affair with the milkman? Men are evolving and this new man cooks a mean shepherd's pie and can change a nappy in 40 seconds! Big up all the stay-at-home dads and big up all the sassy women getting money. Gender roles don't exist anymore you fucking dinosaurs! Go back to Jurassic Park!

WORSHIP HER

I'm one of the biggest feminists you'll ever meet. I think women are goddesses; they are our mothers, our sisters, our grandmothers, our cousin sisters, our aunties, our daughters, our brasses. Women have been treated unfairly throughout human history but times are changing and a gender power shift is taking place. ABOUT BLOODY TIME! AMIRITE LADIES?? Even when it comes to paying the bill at a restaurant, I always insist we split, even if I've had way more than her. Sometimes I'm such an ultra-feminist I insist the woman pays for the whole bill, I'm just a very progressive-thinking geezer like that. To be a Millennial Man you must not only acknowledge that women are our equals but that they are by far the superior race. For all the 'men' who feel threatened by women being equal to us: listen, I would call you a pussy but that would be an insult to beautiful vaginas worldwide, and I love vaginas. They're my favourite human organ just behind the gooch (google it).

HOW TO BE A
LOVER

I was doing some research into my family tree and apparently my great-great-great-great-grandfather invented the solo *Kama Sutra*, he was one of the most legendary wankers of all time. His name was Hardeekh G and he used to have 8-hour masturbation sessions, tantric tossing if you will. I too enjoy beating my dick like it owes me money but I'm not a selfish lover, I find pleasure in pleasing my partner – I once performed oral sex on a woman for three hours and wanted absolutely NOTHING in return. Like I said in a previous chapter, I'm a feminist, mate. In this chapter I will be showing you everything I know about sex and trust me, mate, I know A LOT! The G in my name actually stands for G-spot.

'SEX SELLS, MATE.
TRUST ME, I'VE
BOUGHT IT MANY
TIMES MYSELF.'

CHABUDDY G, CIRCA 2012, IN HIS
WORLDWIDE INTERNET CABIN CAFE.

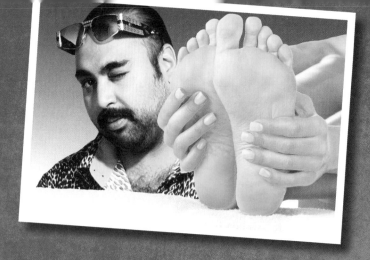

BULLSEYE

Talking of G-spots, did you know that this elusive red isn't just located in her stomach, like I stated in the How to Be a Culinary Expert chapter. Women actually have two other secret G-spots on their body. This is an ancient fact that has been kept secret from fuckboys but because you've bought this book you're obviously a very wise geezer so I will reveal all!

The first G-spot is located on the backside of her left ear lobe, it can only be activated by whispering sweet nothings into her ear while also licking the back of the lobe. You must also have the right vocal tone and vibrato to give her an eargasm.

The second G-spot is very controversial, it's called the foot vagina. Between each toe a woman has a clitoris – it sounds like something out of *Alien* but, trust me, if you find this spot your lady will go crazy. I once deep-throated a woman's foot trying to find it, I nearly gagged and died! It has eluded me thus far but one day I will find it and give a lady the best foot-vagina orgasm ever!

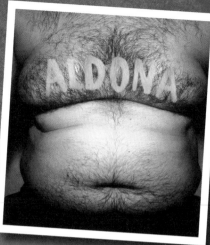

MANSCAPING

Ladies appreciate it when you make an effort. Contouring your body hair not only gives you a more tidy appearance but can also allow you to create muscular definition in places that it might not actually exist. Try giving yourself pecs or a six pack, or those weird muscly bits near your groin that guys have in RnB videos. If you're feeling extra romantic you could even carve her name into it.

THE CHABUDDY G
KAMA SUTRA

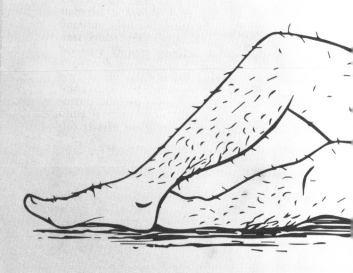

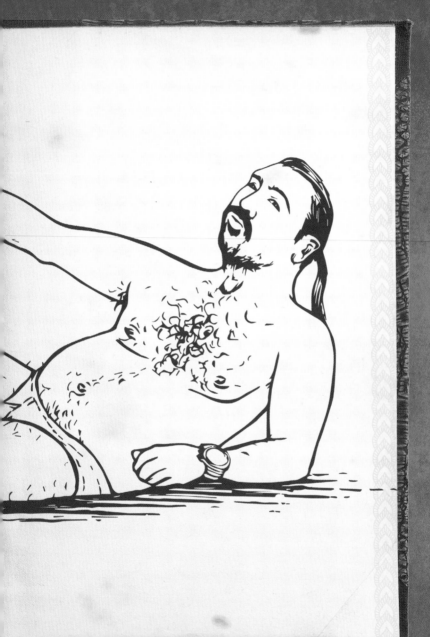

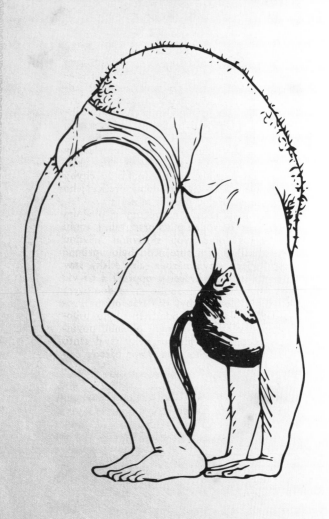

THE SEXORCIST

THE MARILYN MANSON
(NO RIB REMOVAL REQUIRED)

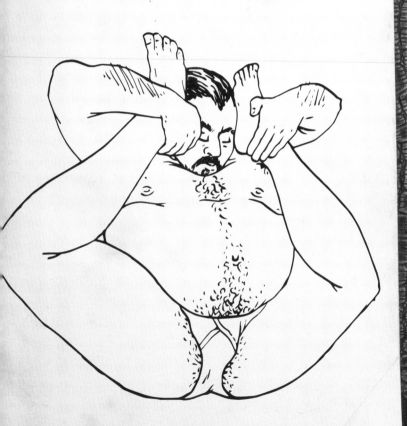

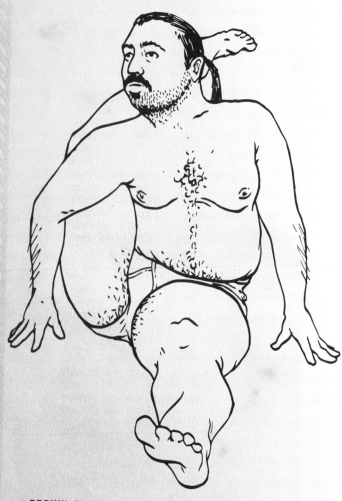

BROWN SWAN

BICYCLE DICK

BE SENSUAL

Being a good lover is all about engaging the senses. Light some scented candles to disguise the smell of rotten peanut dust that's overpowering your bedroom. Spice things up by coming over wearing a curry-flavoured condom! Put a blindfold on her so that she doesn't have to focus on the fact that you're in the back of a van. Keep it sensual and keep it sexy!

ROLE PLAY

If you're struggling to connect with her on a sexual level why not try some role play? Maybe she'll connect better if you tell her that you're an Uber driver with a really bad rating and you need to be punished. Or try breaking into her house unexpectedly and explaining that you're a naughty escaped

prisoner who has forced their
way into her home and needs
help hiding from the police
but also you're very sexy
and she wants to have sex
with you.

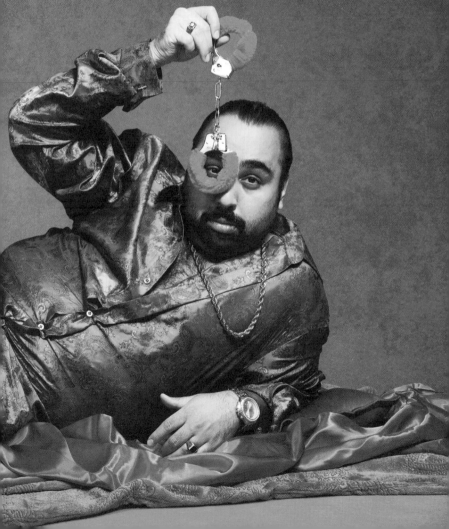

SEX TOYS

Sex toys can really help
add some excitement in the
bedroom, but they also cost a
lot of money. One way around
this is to make your own!
Clothes pegs make excellent
nipple clamps and any type
of belt can be fashioned into
a playful dog lead. You can
even make your own vibrator
by taping a cucumber to a
washing machine and then

putting it on a spin cycle. Apparently. I've never done that. If all of this is a bit too *Blue Peter* for you and you don't have time to be making your own, another thing you can do is buy secondhand sex toys online. These are much cheaper but I recommend washing before use and also getting tested after use.

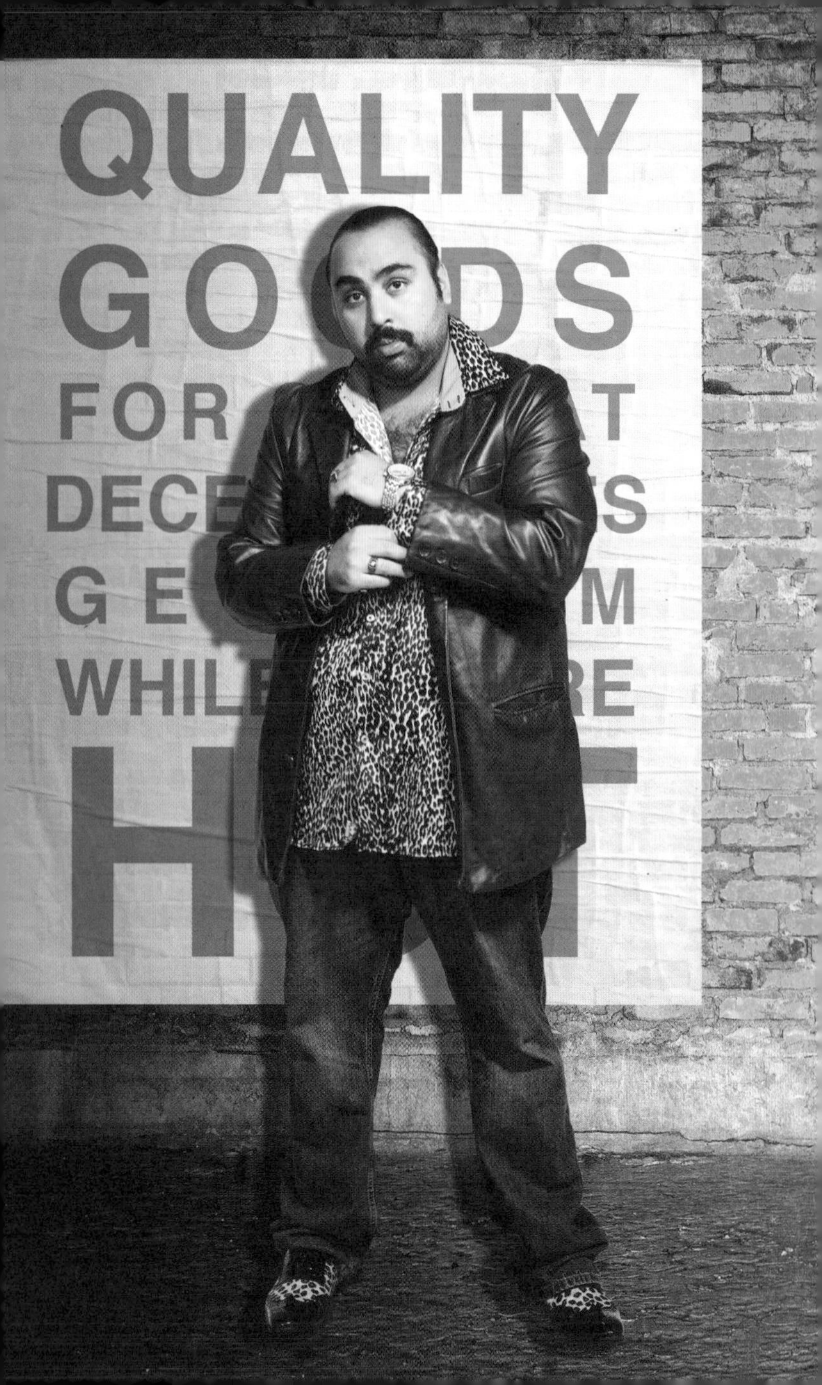
QUALITY
FOR

I remember a great philosopher said 'Once you pop you can't stop'. I take this approach to everything I do – business, inventions, even love.

When Aldona kept on saying she didn't love me, did that stop me giving her money or buying her clothes? No! I'd already popped so there was no way I could stop! Such a great quote. The philosopher went on to create his own crisp range. What a wise ultrapaneer!

The best way to teach you how to be an ultrapaneer is to show you. I'm the ultimate ultrapaneer – I can do it all, mate! So, I'm going to advertise my services and products, and pitch some business ideas just to show you how creative and dynamic I am. I hope you will be inspired – you're welcome!!

Products

£120

SEAN PAUL GAULTIER

It's similar to the normal Gaultier but with a Jerk seasoning twist. Don't be alarmed by the expiry date of 7/3/2014 – this just means it's aged and it is now a vintage cologne. 50ml bottle price: £120.

D&G (DEEPAK & GURDEV)

Two rival cousin brothers, one from Hounslow West called Deepak, one from Hounslow East named Gurdev. For years, their families fought in a bitter feud. Now finally the two cousin brothers have united in the name of fashion. Deepak & Gurdev was born and would change the fashion world forever! I've got 3,076 D&G T-shirts to sell. £45 per T-shirt.

£45

£18.50

PEANUT DUST

You know that bit at the end of peanuts, yeah? Well that's the best part. There was a manufacturing fault where I acquired 3,000 packets of peanut dust, this was back in 2010. I still have 2983 packets left! Peanut dust is multipurpose – it can be used as a facemask, eaten raw, eaten cooked, mixed into drinks, used to clean ovens, mixed with butter to create an unrecognisably different alternative to peanut butter and can also be used as a stimulant for erectile dysfunction by rubbing directly into your penis hole. Watch out for the tiny pieces of glass. £18.50 per packet.

Ideas

SOAP TAP

I'm a busy man, I haven't got time for anything, I'm always hustling, mate! I came up with this genius idea to save time in the mornings. Super-glue a bar of soap to your tap, this way you get soapy water coming directly out of your tap, saves you around seven seconds every day (you will still need to wash your hands later as your hands could potentially get sticky from the soap).

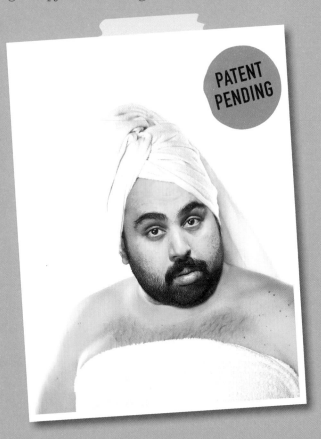

PATENT PENDING

BOOBER

I think there's a gap in the market for an Uber app but for brasses and strippers. Think about it – they have ratings and arrive to your door. All STDs will be listed under info.

PROFIT

$ = ✓

☐ + ⊙⊙ =

BOOBER

SELL

PATENT PENDING

DISPATCHES: FINDING ALDONA

This would be a special investigation following the horrific theft of my Merc and foot spa. I will be playing myself in reconstructions.

IMMIGRANTS GOT TALENT

This is an idea for a TV show that I have – immigrants battle it out for a passport. Judges include Katie Hopkins as the 'Simon Cowell bitch' and Boris Johnson as the 'lovable twat'.

THE GREAT BRITISH VAPE-OFF

Another TV show idea, basically loads of vapists blowing the tonkest vapes and doing sick tricks. Will be hosted by myself and my old flame Mary Berry.

SHOW
IDEA:
£2.7M

Dispatches
FINDING ALDONA

SHOW
IDEA:
WILL DO
FOR FREE

TO GET MY
FOOT SPA
BACK

IMMIGRANTS GOT
T★LENT

SHOW
IDEA:
£4.5M

Services

I am available for work in any of these fields:

SECURITY

I worked as a bouncer at Cineworld, Feltham, for two months in 2008. Got fired because they found out I was a martial arts expert and I was too dangerous to deal with the average man. Hire me and I will make sure no one fucks with you ever again. I can also bring some tonk Polish and Romanian guys.

£250 a day

SEX MAN/GIGOLO

If you can't pleasure your missus then I can and I will. There's a few rules: you can't watch and your lady must be AT LEAST a 3/10. I'm not a prostitute but hard times call for hard moves. Oh yeah, that reminds me, I can't guarantee an erection during love making – it's in the small print, so you can't sue.

£200 a shag

MUSIC MANAGEMENT

Heard of Kurupt FM? No? You been living under a rock, mate? I am Kurupt FM's manager and we have toured in three major cities now, including Ipswich and London. We have 18 genuine listeners every radio show we do and we have a 42-year-old groupie that we have all had a go on. If you want this lifestyle and you're into music, let me manage you.

45% of your earnings

URGENT APPEAL

My book company 'Lady m8 Press' was having cash-flow problems so I partnered up with this company, Harpreet & Colin. I never met them but I think it's some Indian woman and a geezer called Colin. The problem is I've written this whole book and I haven't been paid a penny yet! They promised me 10p per word and this book is 13,000 words, so they owe me £300!

Please, Please, PLEASE contact me, I'm really broke, I've been living in my wan and shitting in a bucket.

Oh yeah … HARPREET AND COLIN, I'M GOING TO SUE THE SHIT OUT OF YOU! I WANT MY 300 QUID NOW!! I'M SENDING YOU PACKAGES FILLED WITH MY HUMAN EXCREMENT FROM MY BUCKET EVERY WEEK UNTIL I GET PAID.

'All good things must come to an end, otherwise how would we know if they were any good or not?'

CHABUDDY G, CIRCA 2016, TO AN AUNTIE AFTER HE PREMATURELY EJACULATED AFTER 8 SECONDS.

SO THIS IS IT.

We have come to the end and, hopefully, we came together. You are now the complete man! Congratulations, look yourself in the mirror and admire the absolute LAD you see before you. I have taught you how to scam, sing and steal, dress, dance and drink, fight, flirt and fuck! I am not the teacher, though, I will always be a student. I learn new things every day! The most important lesson I want you to take away from this masterclass in masculinity is that there's no such thing as a 'real man' and no one can teach you how to be a man! So in a way this book was completely pointless but I've got your money

now so hahahhah, YOU GOT
ROBBED, mate! Only joking
(kind of, haha). There's no real
guidelines on how to be a man,
it's a tough job, geezer! As a
man you must adapt, be
a social, emotional chameleon
with hands strong enough to
crush a man if need be but
also soft enough to hold your
lady with care and tenderness.

Some of us didn't always have
positive male role models
in our lives to teach us how
to be men. A lot of the time
our women showed us how to
be men, our mothers played
both roles. The wisdom I've
imparted on you has come
from the depths of Hounslow;
I listen and learn from other
godly men and now you are

ME. 2078 XO

part of this elite club of alpha males! It's been emotional, bro! If you see me on the street come and say hello, buy me a Brexit Brandy if you want. We can do some lines of peanut dust, talk about politics and I can sign you up to the Beige Party! Above everything else there's two things you need to do to become an honourable man: don't be a dickhead and keep your balls clean. That's literally it! Good luck, my fellow hairy homies. Put this book down and get out there, in that big benchod of a world; look good, smell good, shag good, be brave, be bold, be kind, and remember always ... to be a man!

CHABUDDY G

HarperCollins*Publishers*
1 London Bridge Street
London SE1 9GF

www.harpercollins.co.uk

First published by HarperCollins*Publishers* 2018

10 9 8 7 6 5 4 3 2 1

Text © Asim Chaudhry 2018

Portrait photography © Jay Brooks. All other images © Shutterstock

Illustrations © Julian Gower

Asim Chaudhry asserts the moral right to be identified as the author of this work

A catalogue record of this book is available from the British Library

ISBN 978-0-00-831420-0

Printed and bound in Latvia

All rights reserved. No part of this publication may be reproduced, stored in a retrieval system, or transmitted, in any form or by any means, electronic, mechanical, photocopying, recording or otherwise, without the prior written permission of the publishers.

MIX
Paper from
responsible sources
FSC™ C007454

FSC™ is a non-profit international organisation established to promote the responsible management of the world's forests. Products carrying the FSC label are independently certified to assure consumers that they come from forests that are managed to meet the social, economic and ecological needs of present and future generations, and other controlled sources.

Find out more about HarperCollins and the environment at
www.harpercollins.co.uk/green

HarperCollins*Publishers* strongly advise that readers do not follow any of the advice, guidance or suggestions provided in this book.
We accept no responsibility for injury, embarrassment, financial loss or illness caused by its content – specifically with regards to the recipes, seduction techniques and business/entrepreneurial guidance. HarperCollins*Publishers* are not liable for any damages.